FREE WILLY FOUNDATION

FIELD GUIDE

to the

ORCA

David G. Gordon

&

Chuck Flaherty

Printed in the United States of America
Second printing 1992
Third printing 1994
Special fourth printing 1995

Cover design and illustration: Dugald Stermer
Text illustrations: © 1990 Kelly Balcomb-Bartok
Back cover photo: Alisa Schulman
Maps: Karen Schober
Composition: Scribe Typography
Whalewatching site data compiled by Emily Hall.

International Standard Book Number: 0-912365-37-4

Sasquatch Books publishes high-quality nonfiction and children's titles
related to the Northwest. For more information about our books contact
us at the following address:

Sasquatch Books
1008 Western Avenue
Seattle, WA 98104
(206) 467-4300
(800) 775-0817

Other titles in the Sasquatch *Field Guide* series:

The Oceanic Society
Field Guide to the Gray Whale

The Audubon Society
Field Guide to the Bald Eagle

Adopt-a-Stream Foundation
Field Guide to the Pacific Salmon

Great Bear Foundation
Field Guide to the Grizzly Bear

Oceanic Society Expeditions/Earthtrust
Field Guide to the Humpback Whale

Western Society of Malacologists
Field Guide to the Slug

Contents

Introduction

To the Haida Indians of the coastal Northwest, they are the *Skaana*, the supernatural chiefs of the world beneath the sea. To scientists, they are *Orcinus orca*, the largest member of the dolphin family and the uncontested top predator in all the earth's oceans. To whalewatchers, they're orcas, or killer whales, streamlined animals with glossy black-and-white markings and distinctive dorsal fins that tower nearly 6 feet (1.8 m) above the waves.

No matter what you call them, orcas are spectacular animals to behold. As they patrol the marine waters of the West Coast in family groups called *pods*, the orcas' sleek, almost smug self-assuredness sets them apart from any other breed of mammal. For the authors of this book, their charisma acts as a lodestone, drawing us back each summer to the San Juan Islands of Washington State. Launching our boat from San Juan Island, the second-largest island of the group, we set out each year to reacquaint ourselves with the whales that call these waters home.

Scientists have been observing orcas here in their natural surroundings for nearly 20 years. Each year more and more people join them, making their way not only to the San Juans but to places like British Columbia's Telegraph Cove, Prince William Sound in Alaska, and even California's Point Vicente, specifically to get a glimpse of *Orcinus orca* in the wild.

But orcas have not always drawn cheers from appreciative throngs of whalewatchers. Thirty years ago, sportsmen in Campbell River, B.C., complained so loudly about local orcas eating salmon and threatening the safety of boaters that a machine-gun was installed overlooking the Strait of Georgia to kill or drive away the whales. Fortunately the gun was never fired.

Today the bias against orcas has nearly disappeared from the West Coast, thanks largely to the work of a handful of regional whale researchers. The findings of these dedicated individuals have helped us understand the orcas' ways. In the process, our fear has been replaced with regard for the intelligence, adaptiveness, and spirit of these magnificent animals. To these researchers we dedicate this book.

Having spent weeks at a time in pursuit of orcas, we have learned that any animal that can swim 100 miles in a day is quite capable of making sudden appearances and disappearances. Thus we can hardly guarantee that reading this book will automatically result in whale sightings. We hope, however, that the book will help you understand and appreciate what you're seeing the next time you meet a pod of these wonderful creatures.

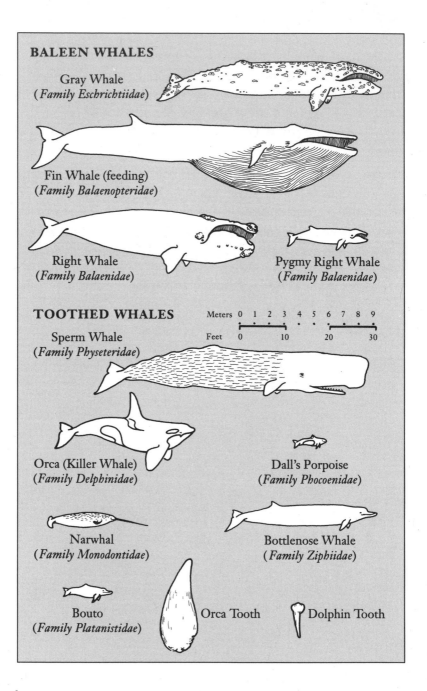

BALEEN WHALES

Gray Whale
(*Family Eschrichtiidae*)

Fin Whale (feeding)
(*Family Balaenopteridae*)

Right Whale
(*Family Balaenidae*)

Pygmy Right Whale
(*Family Balaenidae*)

TOOTHED WHALES

Sperm Whale
(*Family Physeteridae*)

| Meters | 0 | 1 | 2 | 3 | 4 | 5 | 6 | 7 | 8 | 9 |
| Feet | 0 | | | 10 | | | 20 | | | 30 |

Orca (Killer Whale)
(*Family Delphinidae*)

Dall's Porpoise
(*Family Phocoenidae*)

Narwhal
(*Family Monodontidae*)

Bottlenose Whale
(*Family Ziphiidae*)

Bouto
(*Family Platanistidae*)

Orca Tooth

Dolphin Tooth

A Word About Whales

Until recently, mariners as well as landlubbers shared in basic misconceptions about whales. Even Herman Melville, author of the 19th-century whaling classic *Moby Dick*, was unable to tell the difference between the warm-blooded subjects of his book and the cold-blooded fish that swam beside them. To Melville, a whale was "a spouting fish with a horizontal tail."

Today, thanks to the work of cetologists, or whale scientists, the distinctions between whales and other sea creatures are clear. All whales, dolphins, and porpoises belong to an order of marine mammals called Cetacea. Like humans, cetaceans are warm-blooded, they breathe air with lungs, and they give birth to live young. Their babies drink milk, as do ours, from the paired mammary glands of their mothers.

Two major suborders of cetaceans currently inhabit the world's oceans. Toothless mysticetes, or *baleen whales*, are seagoing grazers, taking in mouthfuls of seawater and using a screen of baleen, a hornlike material, as a strainer to capture the relatively small aquatic animals that sustain them. The fin whale, the gray whale, and the largest animal to ever inhabit our planet, the blue whale, are all members of this group. The odontocetes, or *toothed whales*, include the sperm whale, the beluga, and the more than 40 separate species of porpoises and dolphins. Orcas belong to this second suborder.

As the name implies, toothed whales have teeth. However, just how many teeth varies considerably from one odontocete to the next. At one extreme are the members of the dolphin family, whose mouths may carry as many as 200 small, cone-shaped teeth. At the other is the narwhal, with only two, one of which is a long spiral tusk that projects up to 8 feet (2.4 m) in front of its face. In the middle is the orca, technically not a whale but rather a dolphin, whose powerful upper and lower jaws are lined on each side with 10 to 12 sharp teeth, curved slightly inward.

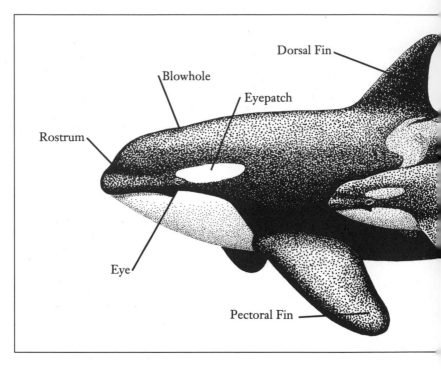

Labels on illustration: Dorsal Fin, Blowhole, Eyepatch, Rostrum, Eye, Pectoral Fin

Orca Facts

SIZE Largest member of the dolphin family. Calves average 7 feet (2.1 m) in length and weigh about 400 pounds (181 kg) at birth; adult females can reach lengths of 25–28 feet (7.6–8.5 m) and weights of 7 tons (6.3 t); males may grow as large as 32 feet (9.8 m) and 10–11 tons (9–9.9 t).

LIFE SPAN Estimated at 50–60 years.

COLOR Glossy black, with distinctive white underside and markings. The shape of the saddle patch, unique to each whale, is used by researchers to identify individual animals.

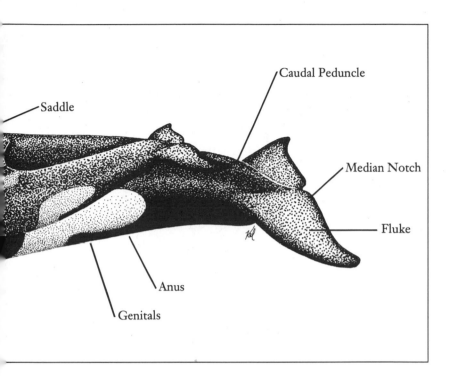

Saddle · Caudal Peduncle · Median Notch · Fluke · Anus · Genitals

BLOWHOLE	Single, crescent-shaped.
FINS AND FLUKES	Full-grown males can be distinguished by their tall—up to 6 feet (1.8 m) in length—triangular dorsal fins; adult females have smaller—less than 3 feet (0.9 m)—sickle-shaped dorsal fins. Flippers of adult males are long and broad, more pronounced than those of adult females. Fluke tips commonly dip downward on adult males.
DISTRIBUTION	Found in all the world's oceans. Range is limited only by natural barriers such as the polar ice pack. Known to gather in large

numbers at the eastern and western edges of the North Pacific Ocean and the North Atlantic, and in Antarctica.

SWIMMING AND DIVING Capable of setting an impressive pace of up to 7 knots and covering 60–100 miles (96–161 km) of ocean in a day. Breathing pattern usually consists of a series of four or more short dives, 10–30 seconds apart, followed by a longer dive of 1–4 minutes. Transients (see page 12) may remain underwater up to 15 minutes at a time.

VOCALIZATION Researchers have been able to identify as many as 62 separate sounds produced by orcas underwater. Frequently recorded are sonarlike clicks, produced in bursts of up to several hundred staccato beats per second, with which the whales are able to navigate and locate prey. Other vocalizations include squeaks, whistles, and shrill calls—sounds used specifically to communicate with other members of a pod.

PREY Members of Northwest resident orca pods apparently favor salmon, herring, halibut, hake, and other fish species. Members of transient pods are thought to feed primarily on warm-blooded prey; remains of over 22 different species of mammals have been found in the stomachs of these whales.

NATURAL ENEMIES Besides humans and other orcas, none.

Orca Society

The basic unit of orca society is the pod, an extended family group of as many as 50 whales. Within the pod are several smaller units called *subpods*. These in turn are composed of even smaller units known as *maternal groups*. In all of these units, the central animals are the females.

Killer whale subpods feed, travel, and cavort together for their entire lives. By observing their interactions, scientists in the Pacific Northwest have been able to compile detailed family trees, tracing bloodlines within orca pods back several generations. We now recognize three distinct pods residing in Washington waters and another 14 pods in British Columbia. A complete census of orca pods in Alaska has yet to be conducted.

Occasionally, two or more pods come together, forming what is commonly known as a *superpod*. Such gatherings often take place during summer and early fall and are possibly related to a seasonal abundance of food. Superpods may also serve a more important social function.

Orca calves are born singly, after a pregnancy that lasts roughly 17 months. The 7-foot-long (2.1 m) newborn begins nursing within hours of its tail-first emergence from the womb. Nursing may continue for over a year, months after the mother has begun encouraging the youngster to accept solid food. Mothers and calves are especially close, seldom separated by more than a few body lengths.

By the end of the first year, the calf will have grown to about 10½ feet (3.2 m) in length. Even at this size, though, the calf prefers to travel at its mother's side. Because many orcas give birth at four- to six-year intervals, it may be a long time before the mother's attention will have to be shared. And in fact, until a female grows old enough to care for her own family (female orcas can reproduce in their early teens), she will rarely stray more than a couple of hundred yards from her mother.

Over a lifetime, a breeding female may give birth to four to six young. Postreproductive females may survive within a pod for over 20 years; it is thought that the role played by such an animal is similar to that of a human grandparent.

One Society or Two?

In recent years, whalewatchers have identified two distinctly different forms of orcas. First are members of what scientists call *resident* pods—families that in summer months remain within clearly defined areas, ranging only about 250 miles in either direction along the coast. Residents come inshore at these times to feed primarily on the salmon that congregate in the narrow coastal passages of Washington, British Columbia, and Alaska.

The second form of orcas makes up what are called *transient* pods. These animals make less predictable appearances, roaming as far as 900 miles along the coast. Unlike the residents, the transients seek larger prey, hunting down other marine mammals—seals, dolphins, and even full-sized whales. Gray whales have been known to roll over on their backs, seemingly paralyzed with fear, rather than fleeing or fighting the members of transient orca pods.

Cetologists have uncovered several other important differences between residents and transients. One is that resident pods usually contain more members than transient pods, which average fewer than a half dozen whales. Also, resident pods vocalize more frequently, using a language of seven to 15 distinct calls. These sounds appear to help the whales maintain pod structure while hunting or cruising. By comparison, the language of transients is terse, consisting of a mere four to seven calls. Transients use this limited language sparingly, presumably to allow them to sneak up on mammalian prey. Transient vocalizations are more frequently heard after an attack.

Scientists suspect that residents and transients seldom if ever interbreed. In fact, residents and transients appear to avoid each other, keeping their distance or even swimming in opposite directions when an encounter takes place. A striking exception to this rule occurred in southeast Alaska when one resident and two transients were seen in joint pursuit of a single porpoise. However, immediately after the attack, the whales returned to their respective pods.

Sounds and Language

Orcas produce sounds for at least two different reasons. One is echolocation. To "see" underwater, all toothed whales emit sound waves, obtaining information about their surroundings from the echoes that return. This information is used in navigation and in finding food. The vocalizations used for these purposes are high-energy clicks; bursts of several hundred are produced at a time.

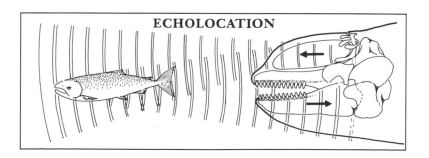

ECHOLOCATION

A second reason for making noise, of course, is to communicate. Orca conversation relies on a repertoire of shrill whistles and high-pitched calls. With these sounds the whales can maintain contact, even when separated by several miles of ocean. Orcas tend to produce more of these kinds of vocalizations as their activity levels increase.

Each resident pod of whales converses in its own distinctive dialect. The calls of the residents of northern British Columbian waters are very different from those of residents from southern British Columbian seas. In sharp contrast, the same dialect is shared by transient whales from Alaska to Monterey Bay, although the calls of transient pods have little similarity to any resident calls.

Scientists have determined that these dialects change little over time. The dialect of one extensively studied pod has remained the same over the last 30 years. In all likelihood, the ability of orcas to communicate with members of another community or another form is quite limited.

Canadian researchers 25 miles (40 km) off the coast of Vancouver Island recently recorded a previously unknown orca dialect. Photos revealed members of a pod never before seen in these waters.

Diet and Appetite

When it comes to feeding, killer whales live up to their name. Strength and a cooperative hunting strategy enable orcas to feed on nearly anything that crosses their paths. The diet of these animals includes a wide array of sea creatures, ranging in size from small fish such as herring or smelt to large baleen whales such as humpbacks and grays. There are no authenticated reports of killer whales eating humans.

An orca's appetite is substantial. A captive specimen may routinely consume 100 pounds (45 kg) of fish in a day. The 19th-century German zoologist D. F. Eschricht claimed to have found parts of 13 porpoises and 14 seals in the stomach of a dissected orca, and yet another seal in its throat. This extraordinary report was supported by one modern-day cetologist who, when examining the carcass of a beached orca on Vancouver Island, discovered several intact Dall's porpoises in the whale's gullet.

When hunting, orcas are team players, literally driving salmon and other cold-blooded prey into the mouths of pod members. Eyewitnesses in Antarctica report seeing two orcas tip an ice floe, sliding its unfortunate occupant, a sleeping seal, into the jaws of a third whale. One pod of killer whales was even observed harassing a moderate-sized blue whale. The attack lasted several hours, during which time large chunks of flesh were stripped from the whale and eaten. The assault ended when the pursuers abruptly pulled back, regrouped, and changed direction, leaving the blue whale to nurse its wounds.

The Free Willy – Keiko Project

In 1995, a program was begun to help "Keiko," the orca whale who starred in the Warner Bros. hit film *Free Willy*, as well as other dolphins and whales.

"Keiko" is a male orca whale, approximately 16 years of age. Since 1985, he has lived at a Mexico City theme park called Reino Aventura.

Thanks to the support of Warner Bros., Reino Aventura, the Oregon Coast Aquarium, the Free Willy – Keiko Foundation, and many others, a new state-of-the-art, two-million gallon, deep-water pool is being constructed for Keiko's rehabilitation. While at the aquarium, the public will be able to observe Keiko; however, he will not be involved in any shows or performances.

Attempts are being made to determine the exact whereabouts of the members of Keiko's original pod. If his skin condition and other ailments can be successfully treated, and if he can be re-taught all the skills necessary to survive in the wild, Keiko will be returned to his family in the oceans off Iceland.

This would mark the first time in history that a captive orca whale was reintroduced to the wild.

The new facility at the Oregon Coast Aquarium will then be used for the rescue, rehabilitation, and release of other dolphins and whales.

For more information about the status of this project, please contact:

> Free Willy – Keiko Foundation
> Earth Island Institute
> 300 Broadway, Suite 28
> San Francisco, CA 94133

Page 16 of this book is outdated. The following information is from the American Cetacean Society's edition of Field Guide to the Orca. The last paragraph is information from Keiko's website, the address of which is provided for your convenience.

<u>ORCAS IN CAPTIVITY</u>

"Scientific curiosity and the desire to bolster attendance at oceanariums and aquariums around the world have led to the capture and display of killer whales. However, it is only since 1967, two years after the Seattle Marine Aquarium (not to be confused with the current Seattle Aquarium) first tested a technique for capturing these animals in nets, that any public facility has been successful in keeping its orcas alive for more than a year. Steady refinements in capture and husbandry techniques have extended the life span of whales in oceanariums to more than 20 years.

"Like some other members of the dolphin family, in captivity orcas are very responsive to humans, easily trained, and adaptable. Trained whales are also used as research animals, participating in scientific studies of echolocation and other behaviors hard to observe in the wild. Samples of their blood, urine, milk, and exhaled air have provided important information on their energetics and reproductive cycles.

"Perhaps the most significant contribution made by captive orcas has been to help change our perceptions of what were once regarded as 'cold-blooded' killers. Captive killer whales have demonstrated their high intelligence, spirit, and marvelous adaptiveness before audiences of people who under normal circumstances might never encounter a whale at close range."

As our perceptions of whales have changed, though, so has our sensitivity to the idea of confining these creatures. If all goes as planned, Keiko would be the first captive orca to be reintroduced to the wild. Keiko was moved back to Iceland, his homeland, on September 9, 1998. It is the hope of the Ocean Futures staff that one day Keiko will be able to live as a wild whale in the waters of his birth. To keep track of Keiko's progress, check out his official home page at:

http://www.oceanfutures.org/

An Uncertain Fate

The Marine Mammal Protection Act, passed by the U.S. Congress in 1972, greatly reduced the threat that humans pose to the survival of orcas. This act made it a federal offense to harm or harass any whale or other marine mammal in U.S. waters. Whaling, of course, was outlawed, as was the once-common practice of firing bullets at killer whales that strayed too close to fishing lines and nets. Canada enacted its own law in 1970, and has banned all capture of orcas.

Even with federal protection, however, killer whales remain vulnerable to human activity. For one thing, they must share their food resources with more and more humans each year. Declining stocks of wild salmon and other food fish may one day limit the number of whales that can survive in our seas. Along with their food, orcas must share their habitat. Increased boat traffic, particularly in Puget Sound and the Strait of Georgia, is creating new opportunities for clashes between whales and humans.

An even more serious threat to orca health is pollution. Animals living on diets of chemically contaminated fish or other aquatic prey tend to store the contaminants in their flesh and fat. A study of blubber samples from harbor seals in Washington revealed concentrations of contaminants higher than samples taken from harbor seals anywhere else in the world. Exceptionally high levels of organochlorine, a compound that can be deadly to humans in large doses, were detected in three orca carcasses washed onto Puget Sound beaches.

If humans and whales are to continue to coexist, steps must be taken toward making this a cleaner world. Information about what you can do to protect killer whales can be obtained from any of the sources cited at the end of this book.

SPYHOPPING

BREACHING

LOBTAILING

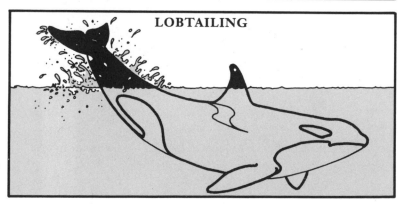

Orca Behavior

SPYHOPPING In a maneuver called *spyhopping*, an orca performs a photogenic tailstand, bringing its head entirely out of the water. This allows the keen-sighted whale to watch for boats, keep in visual contact with other whales, or scan the shoreline for seals.

SLAPPING Sporadically slapping its flukes or flippers against the surface of the water may be the orca's way of herding salmon and other fish. One theory is that the whales drive the fish to the point of exhaustion, then swoop in and devour their frazzled prey.

BREACHING A breaching orca gracefully leaps clear of the water like the star of a gigantic water ballet, then returns to the sea with a resounding splash. Like slapping, this behavior may serve to startle prey—or it may simply be the whale's idea of a rollicking good time.

LOGGING Unlike humans, cetaceans do not breathe automatically. Even sleep, which is characterized by shallower dives and decreased swimming speeds, involves a degree of conscious control. When a group of orcas gathers at the surface and floats motionless, all facing the same direction, researchers call this *logging*. It's a behavior very different from sleep: when logging, the whales may be simply lounging, listening to each other's voices or to the sounds of the sea.

SLEEPING Sleep is characterized by uniform movements: all members of the pod dive and return to the surface at roughly the same time, and each member takes approximately the same number of breaths before diving again. Calves stay close to their mothers' sides in sleep, with the youngest taking the closest berth.

LOBTAILING Also called tail-swinging, *lobtailing* is often an antagonistic display directed at boats or other objects (in one instance a barking dog on shore) perceived by the whales as threats. Orcas can use their powerful flukes like clubs to subdue sea lions and seals; therefore, this gesture is analogous to shaking one's fist. To whalewatchers it is a clear signal to back off and give the whales some space.

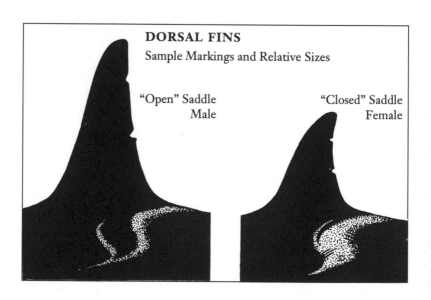

DORSAL FINS
Sample Markings and Relative Sizes

"Open" Saddle
Male

"Closed" Saddle
Female

Orca-Watching from Shore

Watching orcas from shore is a bit like watching sea gulls as they glide past the porthole of a boat. Unless you happen to be at the ready just when the animals cruise by, you may end up spending a lot of time simply staring out to sea.

Your chances of seeing *Orcinus orca* are greatly improved if you confine your efforts to a few special locations and a few months of the year. Generally speaking, the whales tend to stay closer to shore during summer and fall—times when seas are calm and the hunting is best. Still, there are plenty of exceptions to this rule. Whales have been observed entering Coos, Depoe, Yaquina, Tillamook, and several other Oregon bays during April and May, presumably in pursuit of sea lion snacks. Eyewitnesses report chases that have taken the predators several miles up rivers that feed some of these bays.

Observation from shore can be fruitful near Robson Bight, an outcropping of land jutting into the Johnstone Strait in British Columbia. Here, between early summer and late fall, whale-watchers have sighted over 250 of the province's 300 resident orcas. The whales apparently come here to scrape their bellies, backs, and flippers against the smooth black pebbles of the sea-floor. No one really knows why. The bight itself is off-limits to hikers, but other points along this craggy strait afford good viewing.

The only officially recognized outpost for orca-watching from shore is Lime Kiln State Park, on the west side of Washington's San Juan Island. In summer months, when the salmon are most abundant, members of three different pods of whales are likely to swim within sight of the park's conveniently located picnic tables. Island residents claim that the chances of seeing killer whales are exceptionally good—at least one decent sighting every three days. As the pods reverse directions, traveling north, then south, then north again to take advantage of twice-daily oceanic tides, you might even see some of the same whales more than once in a day.

Your chances are best if you have the proper gear. A good pair of binoculars or a high-powered spotter's scope (a monocular viewing instrument available at some sporting goods outlets) easily and comfortably brings the whales into view. Bring warm clothes and rain gear to accommodate any sudden changes in weather, and keep in mind that clear, sunny skies are not a requisite for good whalewatching. In fact, many people feel that overcast days, with reduced surface glare, increase the chances of spying orcas at sea.

Watching Orcas by Boat

Follow the whales' lead and take to the sea and you significantly increase your chances of seeing them. This doesn't mean that you have to own a boat to watch orcas up close: in fact, it's probably in the whales' best interests to discourage the owners of thousands of small craft from forming whalewatching flotillas every time a pod is discovered.

A more humane alternative is to share a boat. Excursion boats operate out of various seaports along the West Coast, carrying amateur naturalists out for mornings or afternoons at sea. Few of these vessels cater specifically to orca-watchers; instead, their captains often prefer to search for seabirds, seals, gray whales, or other more seasonally predictable attractions. However, locating a pod of killer whales is possible, and it's almost certain to prove the highlight of any such journey. When orca pods are in the vicinity, most charter boat operators will adjust their courses to take full advantage of this wonderful show.

Charter excursions specifically geared to orca-watching are offered by Western Prince Cruises on San Juan Island; Victoria, B.C.'s Sea Coast Expeditions; Stubbs Island Charters in British Columbia's Telegraph Cove; Greenpeace Northwest (Seattle); and a few other nonprofit and for-profit enterprises. Fine opportunities are also afforded riders of Washington, Alaska, and Canada ferries. In many instances, these vessels' routes parallel those of whales, and the upper decks of most larger ferries enable whalewatchers to effectively scan the horizon from on high. Larger commercial cruise ships plying the waters of the Inside Passage, Glacier Bay, or other orca haunts in summer offer similar opportunities. The crews of many of these floating hotels include professional naturalists, specially trained to assist passengers in sighting and identifying marine mammals and birds.

For charter boat trips, bring along all of the gear recommended for shore-based whalewatching, plus footwear suited to slippery decks. Also consider taking seasickness medication an hour or two before departure. Don't forget to pack a good field guide to the seabirds and marine mammals of the region, since the chance to see and identify other inhabitants of the killer whale's world should not be missed.

PRECAUTIONS FOR BOATERS

Despite their appearance of aloofness toward humans at sea, orcas are easily disturbed by boaters who encroach on their territory. As a result, the governments of Canada, Mexico, and the United States have passed laws and issued guidelines governing whalewatching craft. Boaters who disregard these guidelines are subject to fines, prison terms, or both. Among the common rules for orca-watching are:

1. Boats should approach orcas slowly, from the side and slightly to the rear, traveling parallel to and at the same speed as the slowest member of the pod.

2. After the whales have been approached, boats should position themselves no closer than 100 yards (91 m) from the whales. Leave it to the orcas to decrease the distance between themselves and you.

3. At no point should boat operators place their vessels between mothers and calves, nor should they perform any maneuver that interferes with the whales' normal behavior. Boats should break with a pod if any whale exhibits evasive, defensive, or aggressive behavior.

Guide to Listings

Listings are arranged geographically, north to south, by state and province. Each listing is numbered for easy location on the accompanying map. Each contains a description of the whale-watching location, viewing tips, and other pertinent information.

Realistically, not every whalewatching expedition will be successful at locating a pod of orcas. Both amateur and professional whalewatchers soon realize that contact with these creatures can be sporadic at best. Watching orcas is just as unpredictable as any other chance encounter with wildlife, and even the best charter boat operators will wisely refrain from guaranteeing sightings of whales.

For a complete, up-to-date list of whalewatching tour and excursion operators, including addresses and phone numbers, send a stamped, self-addressed envelope to:

SASQUATCH BOOKS
1008 Western Avenue, Suite 300
Seattle, WA 98104

In lieu of this list, the following suggestions should prove helpful in locating a tour boat operator:

1. In small towns, contact the tourist information center or inquire in person in the harbor area.

2. In larger cities, consult the Yellow Pages (likely categories include Environmental Associations, Fishing Parties, Museums, Tour Operators, and Tourist Information) or contact a museum. A phone call to the biology department of a local college or university may also produce results.

A final note: Should you know of good whalewatching sites not identified in this book, we'd like to hear from you. Send your tips to Sasquatch Books.

If you have an opportunity to photograph orcas, whale researchers would appreciate viewing your efforts. A good photograph shows the orca's dorsal fin from the side. Photos showing the saddle pattern and eye patch are also useful for identifying orcas. Please send copies of your orca photos to:

Ken Balcomb
Center for Whale Research
P.O. Box 1577
Friday Harbor, WA 98250

Include your name, the location of the orcas, date and time of photo, number of whales (calves and adults) sighted, and what direction they were headed. Please state whether photos were taken from a boat (include boat's name) or from the shore. Please include a phone number where you can be reached.

WHALE SIGHTING LOG

LOCATION	DATE & TIME	WEATHER	SEA CONDITION	# OF WHALES IN GROUP	DIRECTION OF TRAVEL

NOTES:

_____

_____

_____

_____

_____

_____

_____

_____

_____

_____

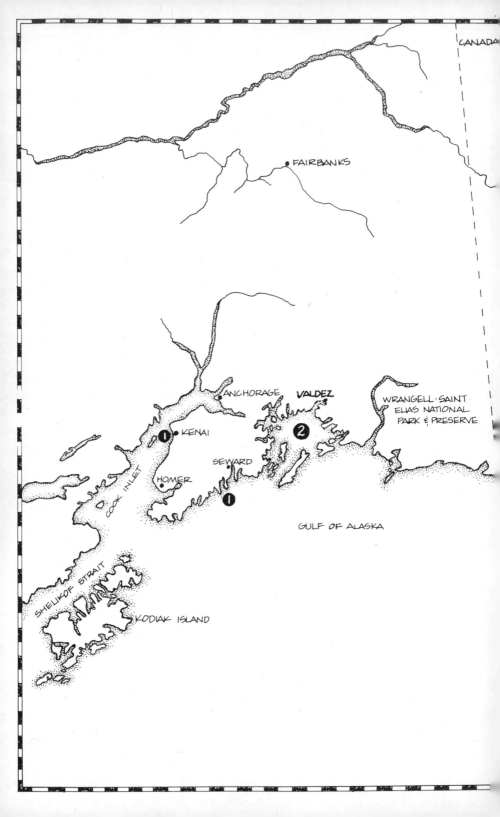

CANADA

• FAIRBANKS

• ANCHORAGE   **VALDEZ**

WRANGELL·SAINT
ELIAS NATIONAL
PARK & PRESERVE

❶ • KENAI

SEWARD

❷

HOMER

❶

COOK INLET

GULF OF ALASKA

SHELIKOF STRAIT

KODIAK ISLAND

Alaska

Both resident and transient orcas are found in abundance in the Inside Passage and the Gulf of Alaska. Alaskans report that the likelihood of sighting orcas is greater here than anywhere else in America. Any sites along these waters can be considered potential observation locales. Unfortunately, getting to them can be a challenge; the vast majority of sites are reachable only by boat or small airplane. As a result, whalewatching by boat may prove more reliable and rewarding. Best bets include the Alaska State ferries or any of the commercial cruise lines that operate seasonally in these waters. Contact the Alaska State Ferry System and the Alaska State Division of Tourism in Juneau for detailed information.

1. KENAI PENINSULA. Nature and glacier cruise boats with naturalists on board leave from Seward and Anchorage each day. Look for whales in July and August in the waters around the peninsula.

2. PRINCE WILLIAM SOUND. Orcas are most commonly sighted from June through September along the west side of the sound. Transients are often observed to the northwest of Knight Island.

3. INSIDE PASSAGE. Whales are frequently seen in the mouth of Glacier Bay (3a), Icy Strait (3b), Chatham Strait (3c), and Stephens Passage (3d). (See map on page 30.) Ferries ply these waters year-round, while cruise ships are frequent summer visitors to Prince Rupert, Sitka, Juneau, Skagway, and Haines.

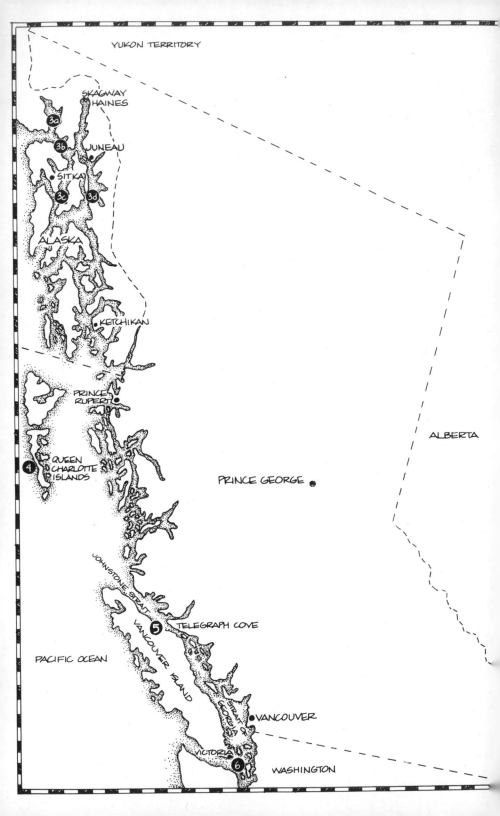

British Columbia

Orcas are abundant along the full length of British Columbia's mainland coast. However, the majority of port cities and driveable roads are found on either side of the Strait of Georgia, making this accessible body of water the best for whalewatching. Whales can reliably be seen farther north in the Johnstone Strait and near the Queen Charlotte Islands during summer months, but getting to these remote outposts requires more of a commitment on the part of the watcher.

4. QUEEN CHARLOTTE ISLANDS. Orcas remain here year-round, but whalewatching by charter boat is generally limited to late spring and summer, when boat operators give tours to see the migrating gray whales. Check ahead if you are specifically interested in viewing orcas. Contact the B.C. Ministry of Tourism for detailed information.

5. ROBSON BIGHT, 15 miles south of Port McNeill from the Island Highway and Beaver Cove Road. The last 2 miles are loggers' road; follow the signs to Telegraph Cove. A protected haven for whales, the bight is closed to travelers on foot. Best bets are charter boats based from spring to late fall at Telegraph Cove. There are campsites at nearby Alder Bay and at Telegraph Cove Resorts.

6. VICTORIA. Several charter boat services are based here. Whalewatching from shore is best at Clover Point and the Ogden Point Breakwater, both on Dallas Road. Approximately 30 miles west of the city on Highway 14 is East Sooke Park, highly recommended by Victoria residents for sighting orcas.

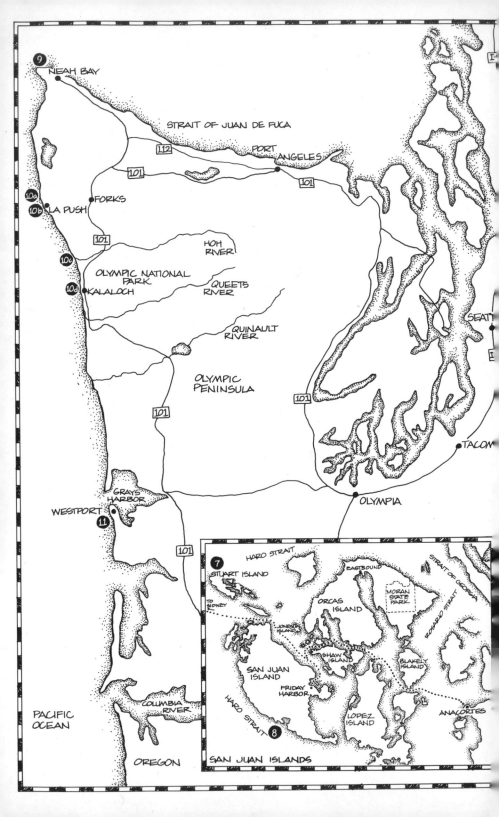

Washington

It's not uncommon to find orcas as far south as Tacoma in southern Puget Sound; however, the whales are sighted with greater regularity in the San Juan Islands. Situated at the confluence of three separate bodies of sea water—the Strait of Georgia, Puget Sound, and the Strait of Juan de Fuca—the San Juans are patrolled by three separate and intensively studied pods of orcas. San Juan Island, one of the largest landmasses in this group, is also the home of the Whale Museum and Lime Kiln State Park.

7. STUART ISLAND. Immediately north of San Juan Island, and accessible only by private plane or boat. The best views are from Turn Point State Park (no overnight camping). Campsites are available at Reid Harbor and Prevost Harbor.

8. SAN JUAN ISLAND. Reachable only by Washington State ferry, small airplane, or private boat. The best onshore and accessible location for sighting orcas in North America. The whales are most frequently seen on the west side of the island; however, the majority of charter boat services depart from Friday Harbor, on the east side.

9. CAPE FLATTERY. Follow Highway 112 west through the Makah Indian Reservation, and follow the signs. Park and walk approximately ½ mile to a series of narrower trails leading to lookout points. (Caution: Trails may be muddy and footing precarious.)

10. OLYMPIC NATIONAL PARK. Main access to the park's beaches is from Kalaloch (10d) on Highway 101, with spur roads leading to coastal areas at Rialto Beach (10a), La Push (10b), and the mouth of the Hoh River (10c). The best viewing points in the park are accessible only to

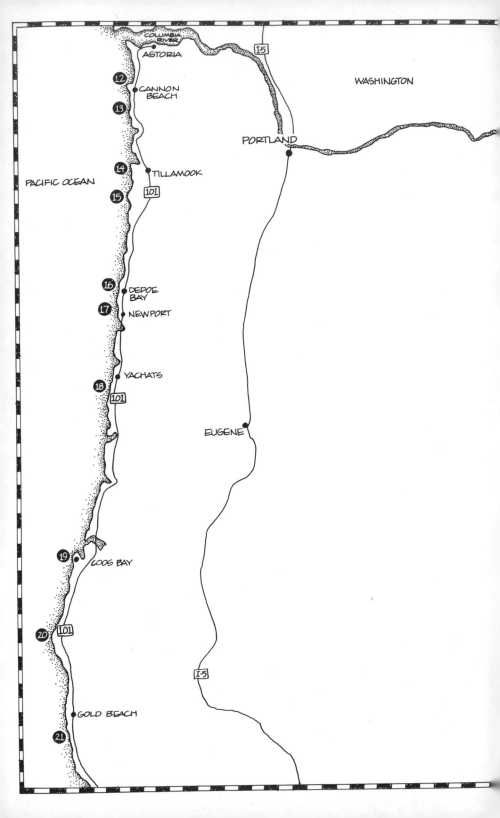

hikers. Contact park headquarters in Port Angeles for information on trails.

11. WESTPORT. Charter boat trips for pelagic bird and gray whale watching are offered in spring and early fall. Of course, the opportunity to view orcas on these trips also exists. Contact the Seattle Audubon Society or the Westport Chamber of Commerce for seasonal schedules.

Oregon

Pods of whales have been sighted entering Oregon's Coos Bay, Depoe Bay, Yaquina Bay, and Tillamook Bay during April and May, presumably in search of sea lions and seals. In recent years such sightings have been most seasonally predictable in Coos Bay; however, the whales appear to frequent different bays during different years. Charter boats (primarily for gray whale and seabird watching) operate out of Newport, Tillamook Bay, Depoe Bay, and Coos Bay.

12. TILLAMOOK HEAD (ECOLA STATE PARK), 2 miles off Highway 101, south of Astoria. Whales can be seen from the observation platform on the south jetty.

13. CAPE FALCON (OSWALD WEST STATE PARK), Highway 101 between Seaside and Cannon Beach. Follow the easy hiking trail to good viewing areas.

14. CAPE MEARES LIGHTHOUSE. Take the Scenic Cape Route (Three Capes Road) from Highway 101 near Tillamook. Unobstructed view of Tillamook Bay.

15. CAPE LOOKOUT, 12 miles southwest of Tillamook on the Scenic Cape Route. A 2½-mile trail leads to the end of the cape, an excellent point for viewing marine mammals.

16. CAPE FOULWEATHER, just west of Highway 101, 7 miles north of Agate Beach. An excellent vantage point with a 270-degree view of the sea.

17. YAQUINA HEAD LIGHTHOUSE (AGATE BEACH). Drive west from Highway 101 (phone the Newport Chamber of Commerce to confirm that the road to the lighthouse is open).

18. CAPE PERPETUA, 3 miles south of Yachats on Highway 101. A short walk leads from the Visitor Information Center to a good viewing site.

19. CAPE ARAGO (CAPE ARAGO STATE PARK). From Highway 101, follow the signs to Charleston or Cape Arago. Several trails lead from the parking lot to viewing spots on the cape.

20. CAPE BLANCO (CAPE BLANCO STATE PARK), west off Highway 101 near Sixes. Drive to a point for viewing near the old lighthouse.

21. CAPE SEBASTIAN (CAPE SEBASTIAN STATE PARK), south of Gold Beach on Highway 101. Take the hiking trail onto the cape for best viewing.

California

With research centers and marine interpretive centers dotting its 840-mile coast, California could very well be considered the West Coast's center for cetacean studies. Much of this interest and activity is focused on gray whales, the predictable long-distance migrants that each spring and fall follow the shoreline between feeding grounds in Alaska and breeding grounds in Mexico. With the exception of Point Vicente, where as many as

EUREKA

CHANNEL ISLANDS

SAN
MIGUEL ISLAND

LOS ANGELES

SANTA
ROSA ISLAND

SANTA
CRUZ ISLAND

ANACAPA ISLAND

SANTA BARBARA ISLAND

SANTA
CATALINA ISLAND

SAN NICOLAS ISLAND

SAN
CLEMENTE ISLAND

SAN DIEGO

22

SAN FRANCISCO

23

MONTEREY

101

PACIFIC OCEAN

SANTA BARBARA

24

LOS ANGELES

25

26

SAN
DIEGO

MEXICO

12 to 15 whales are spied with some regularity, sightings of California orcas are infrequent. However, if you take to the water in search of other sea life, the chances of seeing an individual or even a pod of orcas always exists.

22. POINT REYES NATIONAL SEASHORE. Take Sir Francis Drake Boulevard from Highway 101 to the end or take Highway 1 to Olema and follow the signs. A long stairway leads to the lighthouse, a top whalewatching site.

23. MONTEREY BAY. Well-established shore sites for whalewatching include Point Pinos, Point Lobos State Reserve, Cypress Drive Lookout, and Yankee Point. There are charter boat excursions from Fisherman's Wharf in Monterey.

24. CHANNEL ISLANDS. Ferries from Long Beach, Santa Barbara, and Ventura to Santa Cruz, Santa Catalina, or Anacapa islands. Call Island Packers Co., (805) 642-1398, for ferry schedules and information.

25. POINT VICENTE COUNTY PARK (POINT VICENTE INTERPRETIVE CENTER), on Palos Verdes Drive West on the Palos Verdes Peninsula. SAN PEDRO (POINT FERMIN PARK), White Point at Royal Palms State Beach (Western Avenue and Paseo del Mar). The headquarters of the American Cetacean Society is located high on a cliff overlooking the ocean. A fine spot for watching grays and other whale species. Use the telescopes at the American Cetacean Society's interpretive center to search for the region's resident orcas.

26. CABRILLO NATIONAL MONUMENT (POINT LOMA), south end of Cabrillo Memorial Drive. Telescope-equipped whalewatching platform and glassed-in observatory. Interpretive programs about whales are also offered here.

Suggested Readings

BOOKS:

Barbara C. Kirkewalde and Joan S. Lockhard, *Behavioral Biology of the Killer Whale* (New York: Alan R. Liss, 1986).

M. Bigg, G. M. Ellis, J. K. B. Ford, and K. C. Balcomb, *Killer Whales: A Study of Their Identification, Genealogy and Natural History in British Columbia and Washington State* (Nanaimo, B.C.: Phantom Press, 1987).

Delphine Haley, ed., *Marine Mammals of the Eastern North Pacific and Arctic Waters* (Seattle: Pacific Search Press, 1986).

Erich Hoyt, *Orca: The Whale Called Killer* (Willowdale, Ont.: Firefly Books, 1990).

S. Leatherwood, R. Reeves, and L. Foster, *The Sierra Club Handbook of Whales and Dolphins* (San Francisco: Sierra Club Books, 1983).

James Darling, *Wild Whales* (Vancouver, B.C.: Summer Wild Productions, 1987).

ARTICLE:

John E. Heyning and Marilyn E. Dahlheim, "Orcinus orca," *Mammalian Species*, No. 304 (15 January 1988), pp. 1–9. Published by the American Society of Mammologists.

Information Sources

ALASKA
Alaska State Museum
395 Whittier Street
Juneau, AK 99801

University of Alaska Museum
907 Yukon Drive
Fairbanks, AK 99701

CALIFORNIA
Free Willy – Keiko
   Foundation
Earth Island Institute
300 Broadway, Suite 28
San Francisco, CA 94133

OREGON
Oregon Coast Aquarium
2820 SE Ferry Slip Road
Newport, OR 97365

WASHINGTON
Center for Whale Research
P.O. Box 1577
Friday Harbor, WA 98250

The Whale Museum
P.O. Box 945
Friday Harbor, WA 98250

BRITISH COLUMBIA
West Coast Whale
   Foundation
1040 W. Georgia Street
Suite 2020
Vancouver, B.C. V6E 4H1